William

They say you can never tell
a book by its cover

but when the cover illustration
is this good its a great start
to what will hopefully be a
great book!

Many thanks

Ni~

April 2005

Cover Illustration by William Grandison

Printed in Victoria, BC, Canada

Note for Librarians: a cataloguing record for this book that includes Dewey Decimal Classification and US Library of Congress numbers is available from the Library and Archives of Canada. The complete cataloguing record can be obtained from their online database at:
www.collectionscanada.ca/amicus/index-e.html
ISBN 1-4120-4837-0

TRAFFORD

This book was published *on-demand* in cooperation with Trafford Publishing. On-demand publishing is a unique process and service of making a book available for retail sale to the public taking advantage of on-demand manufacturing and Internet marketing. On-demand publishing includes promotions, retail sales, manufacturing, order fulfilment, accounting and collecting royalties on behalf of the author.

Offices in Canada, USA, UK, Ireland, and Spain
book sales for North America and international:
Trafford Publishing, 6E–2333 Government St.
Victoria, BC V8T 4P4 CANADA
phone 250 383 6864   toll-free 1 888 232 4444
fax 250 383 6804   email to orders@trafford.com

book sales in Europe:
Trafford Publishing (UK) Ltd., Enterprise House, Wistaston Road Business Centre
Crewe, Cheshire CW2 7RP UNITED KINGDOM
phone 01270 251 396   local rate 0845 230 9601
facsimile 01270 254 983   orders.uk@trafford.com

order online at:
www.trafford.com/robots/04-2645.html

10   9   8   7   6   5   4   3   2

To Hippo

Golf and the 8 P of a Logistics Mindset

NIGEL WING

Golf
and
the 8 P of a Logistics
Mindset

Golf and the 8 P of a Logistics Mindset

Introduction

The word 'Logistics' has started to creep into more common usage in our spoken and written language. Phrases such as "Logistically it's very difficult" or "He works for a Logistics company" can often be heard. But what does this word 'Logistics' mean?

The term 'Logistics' is perceived differently by different people; ranging from transport to warehousing, operations management or distribution and storage; parts procurement; even the management of the complete supply chain and many many more.

The word dates back many centuries and is known to have been used often by Napoleon in the organisation of his various battles across Europe. He considered it key to his many successes and losses.

Even the many dictionaries that exist for the English language are unable to agree on a single definition for the word 'Logistics'. The definition that best covers the everyday usage of the word is

> *'The careful organisation of the details of a complex activity'*

If we take this definition, we see that we are all, to a greater or lesser extent, involved in a

Logistics activity. Be it in the work environment, at home or even during our leisure activities, we can all relate to this meaning of the word 'Logistics'.

However complex an activity may be, we have to be able to break it down into more straightforward issues in order for us to be able to manage them.

The use of a simple tool helps us to do just that. The easier the tool is, the more likely it is to be applied and thus bring about improvements in the organisation of these complex activities.

If it is used often enough, it becomes part our way of thinking, it becomes our mindset.

When logistical issues are analysed, it becomes apparent that they boil down to the same 8 elements. To resolve any logistical problem, it is important to ensure that these 8 elements are fully analysed. To do this effectively, the same 8 elements must be reapplied over and over again. It becomes a repetitive check until no detail is left unverified. It becomes a reflex to systematically analyse the 8 elements in detail.

These 8 elements are known as

The 8 P of a Logistics Mindset.

The Story 'Golf'

It's 7am and the alarm rings. Peter rolls over and hits the snooze button. *Just another 5 minutes,* he thought. As he just dozed off, the alarm sounds again. His wife, Anne, nudges him.

"Come on darling, you planned this day months ago. You need the break from the problems in the factory, so go on, get up and enjoy it."

With a few light grunts, Peter gives his wife a kiss on the cheek and makes his way to the bathroom for a quick shower. This Sunday he plans to play a round of golf with Eynon, the local circuit professional. It was actually a prize he won over 6 months ago but has never been able to arrange due to problems at work.

After grabbing a quick mug of coffee and some slices of toast, Peter takes the car keys and leaves the house.

The drive to the Gorse Park Golf Club used to be a very regular occurrence as Peter is a keen player. He played up to 4 times per week but that seems such a long time ago. Recently work issues have meant that even the Sunday morning game with his closest friends is often missed.

The morning is a typical fresh dawn with a light breeze and very few clouds in the sky. *The slight dew on the grass will be burnt off by 9*, Peter thinks to himself.

As he enters the car park, cars are already occupying the prime locations closest to the changing rooms and the club house. *Better chance to get out quickly if I park near the entrance gates in case the factory calls with yet another emergency*, he thinks to himself. *I'd forgotten how popular this sport is at the weekends.*

Peter makes his way over to the Proshop to sign in. As he crosses the car park, his old friend Derek shouts out,

"Hello stranger! Thought you were missing in action or something."

"I was. Well I still am actually but I could not miss this opportunity to pick up a few tips from Eynon. I would never forgive myself if I let this slip by."

In the Proshop, yet more people come up to greet Peter. Not only is he known in the club, but also in the local community. His company is often in the local press due to his business developments or the support he gives to the Chamber of Commerce.

As he goes to sign in, the Pro's assistant asks him for his handicap card. *I really have been gone too long*, he thinks. *The staff don't recognise me anymore.* As he goes for his wallet, Peter realises that he left it on the mantle piece in the dining room. Seeing her name on her badge he says

"Sorry Cris, but I appear to have left it back at home." *What a disaster,* he thought to himself. "I hope I have not forgotten my clubs or golf shoes!"

"Don't worry. Do you have some other form of identification so I can check your membership? And if you have forgotten something, Stan will be pleased to set you up with some new gear!"

After going back to the car, Peter gets his golf bag out of the boot and checks to make sure that nothing is missing. Luckily everything is there and he heaves a sigh of relief.

"Makes a change," he mumbles to himself.

He sees his mobile telephone on the dashboard.

"Today you stay tucked away in the car." *Golf is to get away from it all and I hate hearing phones ringing and people making phone calls on the course. Such bad etiquette,* he thought.

Checking his watch, he sees he still has time for a bacon sandwich before the planned tee off time of 9h15.

Making his way into the clubhouse, he glances over to the prize board where he sees his photograph and name as ex-captain some 8 years before. Those were the days when his wife thought he lived on the course. His handicap was into single figures and for 3 years running he had been club champion. Those days seemed so long ago.

"Buenos dias, Maria," he calls out as he sees the beautiful Spanish girl who manages the restaurant in the club.

After savouring a bacon sandwich and a coffee, Peter makes his way over to the first tee. Still no sign of Eynon. Then with 5 minutes to go, Eynon appears followed by his caddie Tim.

"Just been hitting a few balls to loosen up. Hi, you must be Peter. It's a pleasure to meet you. I have been hearing so much about you and your business successes in the press recently. May I introduce you to Tim, my caddie?"

He extends his arm to shake hands with them both.

"No, the pleasure's all mine," Peter replies. "And I think you have been having far more success than I over the last 6 months. Where are you now in the European rankings? Top 20? Not bad eh?"

"Yep, 18th actually. Things have definitely improved since that disastrous rookie year 4 years ago. So Peter? Pete?"

"Pete's fine."

"So Pete, what handicap are you playing off?"

"Officially the handicap's 12,2 but due to the lack of practice I am playing to around 16. But the rules are the rules so 12 it is."

"So not playing as much as you would like eh? Wife? Kids?"

"Unfortunately work is going through a few 'Logistics' problems and it means we are a bit disorganised at the moment. I do not know what has caused it but we keep forgetting or missing things. Even this morning coming here I left my handicap card at home. I must have other things on my mind."

"Sounds like my rookie year. I was so excited to be on the tour that I kept forgetting details that became rather inconvenient and embarrassing. Luckily I got that resolved otherwise I would not be where I am today. I would have probably lost my card at the end of my first year."

"You will have to share your secret with me. It may help us in the factory."

"Yeh, no problem. I call it the 8 P. We have a good 4 hours ahead of us on the course so we can run through it together."

"Great. Thanks," said Peter.

"So your honour......"

As they strolled down the first fairway, Eynon congratulated Peter on his drive.

"But I thought you said that you were not playing that regularly. That was a great drive. Bandit!"

They both laughed. *These golf Pros definitely know how to put people at ease out on the course,* thought Peter.

"Just luck I suppose," Peter added.

"There is no such thing. Remember that famous quote by Gary Player 'The more I practice, the luckier I get' ? Well, the more attention I pay to detail, the luckier I get. Well, the less likely I am to make a mistake anyway. And the first step is to have a plan. P for Plan or Planning. A kind of game plan I suppose."

"What do you mean?"

"Look," said Eynon, "on that first tee box, you did not just pull randomly a club out of your bag and whack the ball towards the flag. You have a low handicap so you obviously had a plan."

"Well I suppose so," replied Peter a little confused.

"Of course you did. We all need a plan that includes our overall goal and then we detail how we will achieve it. If we do not have a plan then how do we know where to go? The difference is that some of us only plan the next move whilst others plan many moves ahead."

"Sounds like Grandmaster chess."

"Well, its not just chess but everything really, otherwise we would only see as far as the end of our noses." They both laugh. "Take today for example. My plan was to come here to play with some local businessman called Peter, tee off at a quarter past 9, play the 18 holes to par and then, eat lunch in the club house leaving to be home by 4pm, with the aim to play with the kids before bedtime. If it was a tournament week and I was on the circuit, then, my plan would certainly be different because my goal would be different. Perhaps get to the course the day before for a practice round to familiarise myself with the terrain, shoot 4 rounds over the 4 days of say 3 under par in order to finish in at least the Top 10. Pick up a nice pay check then be back home on the Monday morning. The detail of the steps I will go through to achieve these goals will become clear later but first I have to plan the overall objective."

"I am not sure I totally understand what you mean."

"Well let's take an example from your business. I understand in the press that you have just won a contract to build and deliver 20 systems to a new customer in Scotland before the end of next month. Well, there is your objective defined. Once it is clearly defined, you can then plan the detail to achieve it."

"I get it. 'Do what, where, when, how many, for whom' is the goal and then 'the How' is all the complicated detail. And 'why' will help everybody in my team to understand the reason for doing it," replied Peter.

"I bet it is complicated but without that overall goal there will be no focus. And there is nothing more focalising than that end of the month deadline."

"Oh, I know what a deadline is."

"I am not so sure you do."

"Of course, it's easy. It's the 'when' I have to complete a task."

"But do you really understand the significance of the word 'deadline' as opposed to 'completion date'?"

"What do you mean?"

"Well, 'deadline' really gives importance to the fact that a task has to be done by that time otherwise you are dead. There is no possibility what so ever to complete it later. Take for example tee off times in competitions. If I am not ready to tee off at my allotted time then I am out of the competition. No possibility to tee off at a later time. Very embarrassing if that happens. And it has!"

"Yes, I see what you mean. Sometimes in the factory we miss our planned delivery date to the customer. They don't like it and often it costs us money. In one case, that late delivery was very expensive indeed with penalty costs and probably the loss of future contracts so I think the delivery date should be called the 'delivery deadline' from now on."

"So remember, plan the overall goal and plan the detail to achieve it. And remember to ensure that it is communicated to all your team. It's no good if you know the target and the reasons for achieving it but your team doesn't. You must all be singing from the same hymn sheet. Focused on the same goal."

It is amazing how quickly the pair had advanced by this time. They were already putting out on the 2nd green. Eynon had pared both holes, which was to be expected, and Peter was only one shot over. A clean chip out of the green side bunker having saved a disastrous score.

As they moved over towards the 3rd tee, Eynon wickedly posed the question,

"So what's your plan for this hole?"

"Well on this Par 5, I will go for a par for sure."

"Great. And how do you plan to achieve it?"

"Well, I will drive about 220 yards to just short of that fairway bunker on the left. Then a steady 5 wood to about 100 yards short of the green. Chip on and 2 putts for par. Simple eh?"

"Hey, you have a good plan of how you will tackle this hole. See how easy it is? But have you thought of all the detail that goes into the plan? Let's take the next step. You mentioned that you will drive?"

"Yep, that's right. I will hit a driver about 220 yards."

"Ah, good. It appears you are starting to describe a process. The Process of driving. To do so you have a drive swing and a piece of equipment called a driver. The next shot will be a fairway wood process with a fairway wood swing and a different piece of equipment called a fairway wood. Distinct processes and distinct equipment."

"I get it. Each process is an operation with its associated equipment. Let me try that drive process a second."

Peter takes his club out of the bag, prepares his shot, then drives his ball down the centre of the fairway.

"Great shot," says Eynon, "seems as if that process is working correctly."

As they strolled down the fairway towards their balls, Peter thinks back to the factory. The factory has several manufacturing processes, but as his Quality Director keeps reminding him, the company has many different types of processes. Some industrial, some administrative. From the injection moulding and manual assembly to invoice processing and recruitment.

"It is really important that the process works as smoothly and as controlled as possible. For me, I have to firstly ensure that my equipment is in prime condition. That all the clubs are clean, with no damage to the club face and that the grips maintain their feel. Not just after every game but also before every shot, I have to ensure they are in good condition. This increases the probability that the next shot will be a good shot."

"In the factory that relates to the fact that the moulding machines are in good working condition and well maintained. For that we have a maintenance activity for each machine."

As they reach the balls, Peter jokingly says, "Now for the fairway wood process. A bit of maintenance to ensure the clubs are in good working condition. Then make sure the process is ready with a practice swing. Take aim and ...."

Both laugh as the ball goes flying down the fairway to more or less where it was planned to go.

"Just a little bit of variability in that process as the ball was not exactly where you wanted it to go but still a commendable outcome," said Eynon.

"If only it was that simple," Peter replied. "And I don't just mean the golf."

"Well the second step is to identify that the process is an element to take into account. If we forget it then there is no way we can control it. Remember the 2nd P is P for Process."

As they continue towards the green, Peter's mind drifts back to the problems in the factory; the missed deliveries due to machine breakdowns, processes producing at half speed, even machines not prepared to start up on time so everything had to wait 2 hours while the machines were set up for the production. *Why was it not done beforehand?* he thought, *they should have remembered that that machine needed to be prepared in advance?*

After chipping on to the green and putting out, Eynon turned to his playing partner and patted him on the back. "Well, your plan certainly worked on that hole eh? Good par. Let's see if you can do the same on the 4th."

"With a good plan and a mastered process it will be a cinch!" Peter replied.

The 4th was a short par 3. The green at only 140 yards would not be too difficult but as always the course designer had placed a few interesting hazards around the green to penalise any shot (process) that was not perfectly controlled. The bunker to the front was one of the largest in the region and possibly the deepest too.

Eynon's ball, as always, landed on the green at about 8 feet from the pin. Unfortunately, Peter's ball swerved off to the right landing in a smaller sand trap to the side.

"Well your swing process looked fine to me. What happened? Poor contact?"

"I do not know," replied Peter.

Once Peter had chipped back onto the green from the bunker, he went up to his ball to mark it.

"Damn," he murmured as he placed his lucky penny behind the ball. "The ball is split. I'll have to change it."

"That probably explains why the outcome was not as good as expected. I think you have just found the 3rd P. P for Parts."

"What do you mean? Tell me more."

"I'll tell you on the next hole. Be patient and no that is not the 4th P, even though it is a good trait to have."

"So come on Eynon, spill the beans," Peter eagerly asked as they prepared themselves on the 5th tee.

"Well, the 3rd P stands for Parts. For me that can mean the ball. No ball and the process can not produce the shot. It's a key input to the process. Firstly I have to ensure there is a ball teed up ready. Could you imagine how stupid I would look if I lined up to take a shot and forgot to put the ball on the tee?"

They both laughed.

"The quality of the ball has to be acceptable too. Take that last tee shot of yours," Eynon continued, "the ball was either defective before you hit it or it was damaged during the process of the shot, thus resulting in the poor outcome and it certainly would not have helped the next shot either."

"I see what you mean. In the factory we have to make sure the parts are delivered to the process on time and that they are defect free. Remember that expression 'Garbage In Garbage Out' used by computer guys? Well it applies to any process. The quality of the parts going into the process must be of an acceptable standard otherwise the output will not be the desired result."

Peter again started to think of the issues of the last few days in the factory. He didn't want to say too much but he was actually suffering from suppliers delivering late and twice during the last week, the parts received were not to the specification that had been ordered. It was as if nothing had been delivered at all because those parts could not be used by production.

He also thought back to the last inventory check that was undertaken just before the year end. It was amazing the amount of parts that were in the stores which were ordered by mistake or over deliveries that had been accepted. Even they found material that was out of date and was still being held 'just in case.' *Just in case we open a local museum*, Peter thought to himself.

Certainly the parts activity needed some improvement.

Lost in their thoughts, Peter and Eynon had played the 5th hole both scoring a par. On the next tee, the pair had caught up with the group in front who had just finished their drives and were about to walk off down the fairway. Seeing the pair arrive, they stopped and greeted them.

"Lovely day for it," called out Tony.

"Certainly is," replied Peter. "How are you these days Tony? Retirement treating you well?"

"Fantastic. Never played as much golf in my life."

"He has even managed to lower his handicap 4 strokes in the last 6 months. Can you believe it?" added one of the other players.

Tony was an old friend who had worked in the same factory as Peter but just over a year ago he started his retirement. He had been part of the company management team that had started to develop the new product line but was not able to see it through to launch because his wife insisted very strongly that at 65 he was to retire to be at home with her. Little did she know that his golfing passion would again keep him away from her. "If you can't beat 'em, join 'em," she had said, so she too became more active down the club and was now a regular player in the ladies seniors' team.

"Oh, how can I be so rude? Gents, let me introduce you to Eynon and his caddy Tim," said Peter remembering that his playing partner had not yet been presented.

"The one and only eh? You giving a few lessons to young Pete this morning? He certainly needs a few tips," added Thierry also thinking of his own game.

"His golf is just fine," Eynon replied. "He just needs to practice and get his mind focused on his game."

As good etiquette dictates at moments like this, Tony offered to let the pair play through as their fourball had lost ground on the group in front.

Peter and Eynon both played their shots down the fairway and even received a round of applause from the group watching.

As the twoball walked off, Tony called out,

"Pete, you can fill me in on the factory when we get to the 19th."

Peter nodded his head in agreement.

Peter again drifted off back into his thoughts but this time was recapping what Eynon had so far explained to him.

Before I start to do anything I need to have a clear objective so I can ensure that all are focused towards the goal. It needs to be clearly described. Then I can start to plan the detail of how.

The processes are what will transform the parts but.... just a minute; processes need people to operate them. None of my processes work completely automatically. There is always someone operating the machine or doing the filing. Well, that is when the supervisor remembers to put the person at that workstation. If not, the machine does not run.

"Hey Eynon, I think I have the next P!"

"Just let me finish taking this shot, then you can bounce it off me."

Eynon's ball, as always, was headed straight for the green.

"Nice shot. I wish I could have done that."

Eynon handed his club to Peter and then said,

"Okay, your turn. You do it."

"But...."

"No buts. Just do the same swing, I'll give you the same type of ball in just about the same position. Give it a try. Nothing to lose."

Peter took his swing and the ball shot down towards the green but was a good 30 yards short.

"But that demonstrates exactly what I want to say."

Peter was getting quite exited as he knew that he had come up with the next P.

"P for People! The 4th P is for People."

"Well done," added Eynon. "And not just for the 'P for People' but also for the good shot. It was quite a difficult lie."

"I think that the people element is quite important 'cos they are the ones who operate the process," Peter started to explain his thoughts. "Not only do they have to be there, physically present, but they also have to have the correct skills. Take that last shot for example, I was there to make the process work but I do not have quite the same skill level as you so the outcome was not the same as yours."

"The skill factor does play a role but the level of skill required depends upon the process that needs to be performed. Take, for example, a putting process. Firstly the person needs to be physically present to hold the equipment and perform the process. Then he needs to have a minimum level of skill in order to hold the club correctly and to do the correct stroke. This will at least guarantee the basics and will probably be effective on say a 2 or 3 foot putt. Then yes, if the putt was let's say 20 feet or more or the green was tricky to read, this is where the skill element would really come into effect. I suppose it is the difference between a 2 or a 3 putt."

"In the factory, the machine operator has to be able to load and unload the parts and to run the machine. It's true, in some processes the 'skill' required is considerably less than, for example, the guys in our prototyping department. These guys really are skilled craftsmen, with years of training and practice."

"Horses for courses my old chap," Eynon chuckled. "But just make sure you remember to always check the people element every time. Later I will tell you something that helps me to do that."

The pair was playing a good round of golf. Not only were they scoring well but also playing at a good pace. The 6th hole was played in par again and the drives down the 7th were in a prime position for chips onto the putting green.

The sun was rising and had burnt off most of the dew on the grass so the ball was beginning to roll further and the putting was easier. The only dew what remained was in the shadows cast by the trees lining the fairways.

Peter remembered when he first joined the club as a youngster. The trees had matured considerably over the past years and were a constant reminder to him of his advancing age. Being a course that was surrounded by farm land, it was often that rabbits and even pheasants could be seen roaming fairways in the early hours after sunrise. It really is a small paradise to come here and to get away from the day to day life in the factory or city. *I must find a way to get back to my old routine of playing several times per week*, he thought.

Despite the good drives, Peter's score on the 7th was one over par. The chip to the green did not hold and ran off the back requiring a delicate chip and run back towards the flag. But still 2 putts were required.

After finishing to putt out, Peter posed a question.

"We've talked about putting parts into a process and people being able to operate the process, but what about the output or the result. Is it not the Product? P for Product?"

"Exactly. We have just produced a shot. Or produced a putt. The Product is the result of the process. It could be a good product or a not so good product. Remember your shot that swerved away on the 4th? The product of your process or should I say the shot that resulted from your drive was not as expected because of a defective ball. The final product was that you landed in the sand trap."

"And I suppose if the person was not trained correctly the shot would also be poor. Well, if I look at our factory, using poor parts, poor people, people not trained adequately I mean, and poor process, always results in poor product."

"Don't focus on the poor aspect. Be positive and think good parts, good process, good people etc. In golf you have to have this positive perspective. You have to ensure that things are correct i.e. check that the ball is ok, check that the club face is clean, check the grips are ok and check the swing is correct with a practice swing. You have to prevent that it is wrong."

"I know pessimism is not good. So, good parts go in to a good process operated by good people and good product comes out. I have to make sure they are all good then the product is virtually guaranteed to be good."

"Well not just the Ps we have talked about so far but also all the Ps to come. They all have to be good otherwise the plan will not be achieved correctly. But just keep thinking positively. Always ask yourself 'What do I need to do to ensure that it is good?' "

As they made their way to the next tee box, Tim, Eynon's caddie, finally joined the conversation.

"The next P is one which I am very much involved in," he said. "It's what we call P for Placement. Basically it means ensuring things are in the right place at the right time. For example, at this moment it is my role to ensure the clubs are moved to the next tee and that they accompany Eynon around the course. And giving him the ball before teeing off. If I look more globally, one of my responsibilities as caddie is to ensure my boss gets from the hotel to the course on time. I even organize the flights and the hire car. All actions of placing Eynon in the right place at the right time."

"I see what you mean," replied Peter. "I suppose it's like our company ordering the parts from a supplier but forgetting to transport them to the factory. Or even worse, having them in the warehouse but not placing them near the process so they can be used."

"Or having produced your product for the customer, leaving them in the finished goods warehouse and forgetting to deliver them," added Eynon.

Peter looked at him and laughed. But it was one of those laughs that showed that he was touching a nerve. *Has he been speaking to someone at the factory?* Peter thought as this had not that long ago happened to a shipment. Everyone thought that someone had organised the transport but in fact no-one had. Such embarrassment when an angry customer phoned to complain that his product had not arrived and then after checking, realising that it had not even left as everyone had dangerously assumed.

"Yes," Peter replied finally. "Placement, as you call it, is quite a subject. It can also be quite complex and complicated. Moving parts or people is not always as predictable as you would think."

"You do not have to tell me," added Eynon. "Flight delays, traffic jams, cancellations, etc"

"Add to it Customs and Immigration procedures then in some countries you are entering into a big unknown."

"Exactly, the delays are really unpredictable. When I take a flight, I make sure I arrive a good 2 hours before the take off time as I know in some airports there are big queues through all the controls. And again when you arrive in some countries, its absolute chaos too."

"Well, when we send our lorries around Europe, things have improved tremendously in the last decade but if you go into Eastern Europe then the border controls can add nearly a day to the transit time depending when you join the queue."

"I do not know whether you experience the same in your company Peter, but there are also times when the choice of transportation is also important depending upon the distance required and the time available."

"Not to mention the cost."

"Sometimes its best to take a car instead of a flight as the total journey time is actually quicker when you take into account the waiting time, controls etc."

"Even the choice between motorcycle and car for getting through the traffic to deliver a parcel or documents. In some big cities they do this kind of delivery by bicycle as it's quicker for small packets. But one thing is for certain, the quicker you need to get something from A to B the more expensive it becomes. And it's exponential!"

"As in the other cases, it's important to take the P for Placement into account and not ignore it. Brainstorm all the scenarios possible."

"It reminds me of that film with the late John Candy 'Planes, Trains and Automobiles' but you need to change the title to 'Planes, Trains, Automobiles, Motorbikes, Ships, Bicycles and Shanks' Pony' to cover all the options. Well, that's not all but you know what I mean."

Both Peter and Eynon continued to talk about there travel experiences. Traffic jams in the big cities, Airport strikes, delays, missed flights, road works, … you name it, it had happened to both of them.

By the time they had finished talking about different types of planes and cars and other means of transport that are common in today's world, the pair had played through to the 12th hole. The game had, as for many a person who plays the game, become a very sociable event whilst walking around the course. Both were really enjoying each others company and even Tim was becoming more involved in the conversation than at the beginning.

It was Tim in fact who brought them back to the topic of the 8 P when he complained that the luggage had often been delayed in airports and even once did not arrive in time for the start of a tournament in Scotland, the home of golf.

"Well, I think I've just given you a clue about the next P," said Tim.

"What do you mean?" replied Peter.

"When I mentioned about the luggage, I nearly called it Packaging."

"I get it. P for Packaging"

"You see, the packaging element is also very important. Firstly, the parts come in packaging, the clubs are carried in packaging and when we send the clubs by plane, we place the whole lot into another packaging, a travel bag, to ensure they are not damaged. All our clothes are packed in suitcases for the travel. You see, Eynon and I always refer to it as packaging, and not luggage, because of the 8 P."

"I get it. Packaging is important. Some of the parts we purchase come very well packed to ensure they arrive without any damage and there are also sub modules so they can be placed directly onto the assembly line. A bit like your golf bag being placed inside a travel bag. Then there is our finished product that when it is sent overseas gets a different type of packaging from that which is sent by road to a customer about 100 miles away."

"Well, for packaging, you could also say our clothes are included because it is packaging for people! Different days, different clothes. For sunny days there are clothes that keep us cool."

"And waterproofs to keep you dry on typical wet and windy days!"

"Exactly."

"I see that these Ps are very much applicable to every type of situation. You see in the factory our people also need correct packaging. In the paint booth they have protective clothing and in the goods inward reception area they have warm waterproofs as the forklift trucks often operate outside. Even the sales force has a uniform so that when they visit the customer they can be easily recognised."

The 13th, a short par 3 was played without any serious difficulties by either player. They both were on the green with 2 puts for par. Although Peter misread the green and left his ball short and left of the hole, he managed to sink the remaining 5 foot putt for par.

On the 14th tee, conversation was still on the packaging element. As they drove off down this long par 4, Peter asked,

"Come on, so what's the next P?"

"Well, what have we seen so far?"

"P for Plan, P for Process, P for Parts, P for People, P for Product, P for Placement and P for Packaging; 7 so far. Come on, what's the last one?"

"OK then. The final one is P for Paperwork."

"Paperwork?"

"Yes, paperwork. For example, for me an important piece of paperwork that I must always have with me is my professional license. And when out on the course I must ensure that the score card is filled out correctly, checked and then signed before I give it in."

"Paperwork could also be the airline tickets for the flight," added Tim.

"And passports, with a visa," Eynon said as he slapped Tim on the shoulder.

"I know, I know. You will never let me forget that will you?" replied Tim.

"What happened? Spill the beans," enquired Peter.

"Well, I forgot to check whether we needed to apply for a visa before we went to India and they stopped us from boarding the plane because we did need one and I hadn't organised it. So embarrassing."

"I can see the importance of this now. It's like all the customs documentation for exporting or importing goods. You could get everything to the local airport, then it's blocked there because it misses the simplest of documents. Or as you say, forgetting your passport, or it being out of date, will stop you from being able to take a flight. All the other P's could be perfect but forgetting your passport puts the kibosh on everything."

"It certainly does."

"I also think that the paperwork may be very much linked to the other elements. For example all our processes have their paperwork. The work instructions so that the people know how to run the process and also the maintenance instructions for our maintenance department. We have seen the paperwork for the placement element; tickets, customs documents or passport and visas", he said as he winked to Tim.

"I tell you, I will never be allowed to forget this. Eynon always finds a way of bringing it up in conversation," Tim moaned.

"Paperwork for packaging i.e. the packaging instruction or packaging labels; paperwork for product i.e. a user manual or even serial labels; and paperwork for the planning could be the schedules sent to suppliers or a flow diagram of the steps to be taken or a Gantt chart."

"I like how you have just joined that P with the others 'cos it can be done to a greater or lesser extent for all the elements. Remember when I said to you about a system for ensuring that nothing has been forgotten? Well I think you just applied it? For each P, you apply the other Ps again," Eynon explained.

"I'm not sure I follow."

"Yes you do but let me structure it better for you. If I said to you People Paperwork or Paperwork People what do you understand differently for these 2?"

"Well for me, People Paperwork would refer to perhaps the documents that the people require, i.e. passport, Social Security documents, tax forms, work permits. Whereas Paperwork People would be those people that deal with the paperwork. In the factory that would be Kate and Marie in the accounts department processing the invoices or perhaps Karen and Val who prepare the dispatch paperwork before every shipment."

"Exactly. They are different but each one helps remember more detail. In fact there are 2 ways to check. For example, either to check the People aspect of all the other elements or to fully check the People element itself. It does not matter which you do first as you will check both ways in the end."

"Sounds a bit complicated."

"Not really. It makes it easier to say out loud 'the' before each one. So here is the first check:-

      The Planning People
      The Process People
      The Parts People
      The People People
      The Product People

The Placement People
The Packaging People
The Paperwork People

As you can see here we are looking to see which People are involved in ensuring that each of the other elements is undertaken correctly.

In the other case, we check the People element with the help of all the other elements:-

The People Planning
The People Process
The People Parts
The People People
The People Product
The People Placement
The People Packaging
The People Paperwork

Let me take each of those one by one and see if you can give an example for your factory."

Eynon looked at Peter to see if he was following. Peter nodded his head in acknowledgement.

"So, the Planning People, what do you think?"

"Well, I suppose it is the people who do the planning. The guys and girls of our planning department."

"Good. What about the Process People?"

"All the people that are required to run the process and maintain the process."

"So far so good. What about the Parts People?"

"That must be the guys who are there to order the parts from the suppliers and to get the parts into the factory and to the lines. But would that not be better to say the Parts Placement People or the Parts Planning People?"

"Yes, you are quite right. It is possible to go deeper and deeper but let's just concentrate on step 2 for the moment. We will not go through every one but what about the Placement People?"

"Well that could be the lorry driver who will transport parts or product, even the forklift driver who moves the parts or product within the factory. It could also be the airline pilot who flies the plane."

"I think you are getting the hang of this. Try this one. It has often stumped Tim but is actually something very important; the Placement Paperwork?"

"Come on now. Give me a break about the passport and visa. You also forgot your tickets many years ago but I do not remind you every 5 minutes, do I?" added Tim.

"Sorry but I could not resist," said Eynon. "Well try this one then. The People People? When we are on tour they are very useful as they really make life easier for the players. There is a whole organisation of people to take care of the players and caddies and ensure we are ok."

"We have a whole department in the factory who are the People People. You could say that our Human Resources team are the People People. They are there to coordinate the recruitment of the people and the training of the people. The medical team are also People People. I should also say that to a greater or lesser extent, every manager or supervisor is a people person as part of their role is people management," replied Peter.

"Well done. I see that you have really got the hang of this."

"To be honest, it seems so simple. Even common sense. But you know what they say that these things are only obvious once someone has explained them to you."

"I prefer to say the same as Galileo in that I am only brining to your awareness something that you already know."

By this time, the pair, followed by Tim, were coming down the final fairway. The round of golf had lasted over 3 and a half hours but the time felt as though it had flown by.

Just in front of the 18th green, a small stream cut across the fairway thus requiring the final approach shot to be pitched directly onto the green.

Both players found the putting surface and as they walked to the green Eynon turned to Peter and said,

"Peter, you see this little stone bridge we have to cross to get to the green?"

"Yes?"

"Well you see the stones that make up the arch of the bridge? Every stone is a fundamental element to support that bridge. Without any one, the bridge would collapse and we would be unable to cross. To me, those 8 stones represent the 8 P. Miss one and the organisation is doomed to failure."

"I see what you mean."

"Well, when I want to remember the 8 P, I try to picture a famous stone bridge just like this one. I am sure you know the one I mean. It gives me constant inspiration to focus my mind on the 8 P. In fact, I have a painting of the Swilken Bridge on my wall at home and it helps keep that image fresh in my mind and continually remind me of the 8 P. I suggest you do the same."

The 2 players crossed over the bridge and joined their balls on the green. After repairing their pitch marks, both players putted out.

Removing his cap, Peter walked up to Eynon to shake his hand.

"Thank you Eynon, it's been a great round of golf and I have learnt so much about the 8 P."

"It's been a pleasure and I hope it will be of use to you back at the factory."

"Absolutely! I can't wait to get back tomorrow and explain to everyone the 8 P. I am sure that we will be better at organising in the factory once we use the 8 P and create a 'Logistics Mindset."

Logistics Mindset

The 8 P of a Logistics Mindset

'It is not the ability to remember but the ability to organise knowledge.'

Nobody is expected to instantly remember every detail of such complex logistical issues.

What is important, however, is the ability to use a simple structured reiterative thought process to ensure that all the detail is identified, organised and then managed.

The 8 P are the basis of that thought process.

The 8 P are 8 elements that need to be verified in order to ensure all aspects of logistical issues are taken into account.

These 8 elements can be visualised as the 8 stones in the arch of a bridge. All 8 elements are important. If they are all analysed in detail then the arch will be solid and the bridge will be strong.

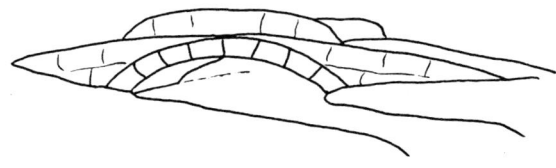

If an element is not analysed sufficiently then the arch will have a weak element and the bridge may collapse.

Each element is not to be considered in isolation as all the elements interact and support each other. This interaction will be explained later in the chapter "The Next Level".

Firstly, it is important that the basic concept behind each element is understood.

All elements are applicable to all the different types of organisation that exist. Be it industrial or administrative. Be it professional or personal.

The 8 elements, all beginning by the letter P, are:-

> Planning
> Process
> Parts
> People
> Product
> Placement
> Packaging
> Paperwork

Planning

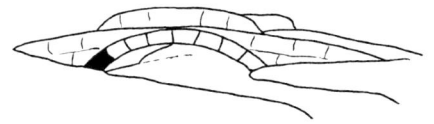

Planning is broken down into 2 stages.

Planning (Part I)

Initially the organisation needs an objective, a purpose, a goal. What we want to achieve, where and when. Be it for the driver to deliver a finished product to a customer before 10am tomorrow, for the assembly line to produce 100 units before the end of the shift or for my son to bake a cake for his mother's birthday party at home this evening at 8 Pm.

Without this goal everything else loses direction, loses focus.

From this point on, we will plan activities and tasks. These activities and tasks will be identified when we analyse the other 7 elements. We will come back to this second stage later. See Planning (Part II).

The definition of the goal should include:-

What – what it is we have to achieve

When – when it should be completed by

Where – where it has to be done

Who – who it is for

Why – why we will do it so all concerned can understand and buy in

How many – the quantity required

Those people who are familiar with 5W2H will note that the 'How' is missing in this definition of the goal. The reason is that the detail of 'How' we will achieve this goal will be detailed once we analyse the other 7 P and come back to Planning (Part II) later.

Process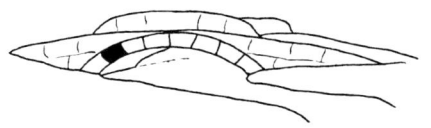

The Process element details the transformation of inputs into outputs.

The Process could be, for example, to place a component blank in a stamping machine which then transforms the part. A stamped product is produced. The Process is therefore a stamping Process and has a stamping machine.

In a kitchen, the chef takes eggs, breaks them into a bowl and whisks them with a whisk to produce a mixture ready for the next Process of frying an omelette in a frying pan.

Alternatively, the Process could be administrative in that raw data is input, it is organised and sorted and the output could be a report or some graphic presentation. In this case the machine that is used would be a computer or data processing system.

Parts, Process and Product go hand in hand. Parts are an input, the Process transforms the Parts and Product is produced.

The Product coming out of a process could then be the Parts that are an input into another Process and so on in a chain.

Whenever the word 'Process' is used, it is important to ask ourselves 2 questions:-

1. What transformation/action is taking place and what tool/equipment/machine is being used?

2. Is it possible to break the Process down into sub-processes?

These 2 questions will allow us to analyse the Process in greater detail.

In all cases, Processes are operations that are undertaken by People and/or machines.

In the 21st Century, the term 'Process' is being used more and more to describe the operations of a company. Quality Management Systems are now orientated in the 'process approach' with inputs, process and outputs. The 8 P is in accordance with this thinking.

Parts

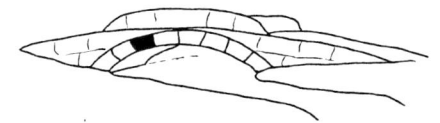

Parts, materials, components, information are key inputs in all processes. In an assembly process, we take 2 or more components and join them together to make a product. In a machining process we take pieces of metal and turn or mill them into new product. A chef takes different ingredients to prepare something delicious. In an administrative environment, the parts would be documents or information or data.

The parts must be correct for the process. If the quality of the parts is bad, then there is a high probability that the product will be wrong. It is always important to ensure that the parts required respect a previously defined standard.

The parts required are often described in a parts list or bill of materials. Some organisations, like restaurants, use the term recipe. If the list of parts is incorrect then this will have an influence on the final product.

Other types of parts which need to be considered are those which are known as consumables. These are parts which will not be incorporated into the final product but will be consumed by the process.

Good examples of consumable parts are oils for engines, cutting blades, or filters in an industrial environment. For other types of industry they could include printer ink cartridges, cleaners' gloves or even the gas or electricity that is used for the chef's oven.

People

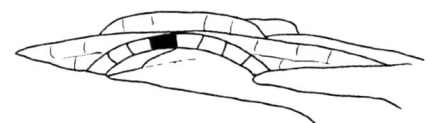

All organisations involve people; ranging from the one man band up to the multinational group. Each person plays a key role in the advancement towards the goal. Without people the big wheel will not turn.

It is not sufficient to have anybody. The people must be correctly trained and in sufficient numbers to fulfil the desired tasks adequately. Often these people will need supervision / coordination to ensure their efficiency.

The human resources aspect of any organisation is subject not only to the rules and regulations of the country in which it operates but also to good business ethics.

Know your people, know their capabilities and treat them fairly. They will be loyal and work with you, not against you.

People are not inanimate objects. If a task is critical to the success of the whole operation or if the deadline is approaching, the organisation becomes more dependable on the ability and motivation of these individuals. It is important that the goal and the tasks are clearly communicated and understood to ensure that all have a clear focus on the job in hand.

Product

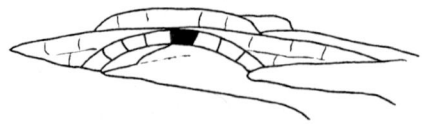

As described earlier, the product is what the process has produced. It is an output of the process.

The product could be a physical item, it could be a service that is provided, it could be information.

In some cases, we not only produce the desired product but we may also produce bye-products. These may be of use to the organisation but more often than not they are product which we do not want and can cause us problems in their disposal.

In order to protect our environment we must manage both product and bye-product in a responsible ecological manner.

The product is not the goal of our logistical problem. It is only one part of the chain. As mentioned above, it is an output of the process. We have yet to get this product to its customer.

Placement

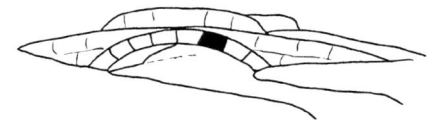

The element of placement covers all aspects of moving something from A to B; be it parts, be it people or be it product. Often they are not in the correct location and have to be moved to be where they are required at a particular moment in time.

The placement element can be considered into 2 major groups. Those activities external to the organisation include the more conventionally understood aspects of transport by land, sea or air. Additionally there are those elements that could be considered internal to the organisation i.e. offloading by forklift, carrying by hand, use of pallet trucks, handling by a robot, conveyors,....

Any other movement from A to B must be considered in the Placement element however small that movement may be.

Even the act of storage is to be considered a Placement element as the product is being placed in a location for a set length of time.

The Placement means must be appropriate for what is being moved and how quickly it must reach its destination.

The different types of transport available are very varied. Often we are able to do the placement by our own means and other times we have to call the assistance of 'specialists' in transportation.

The cost is often a function of the size and weight and inversely proportional to the duration of the journey. A clear example of this is transporting a large box by normal postage is more expensive than an envelope. If we then decide to send it by 24 hours next day delivery then the cost is exponentially more expensive.

Packaging

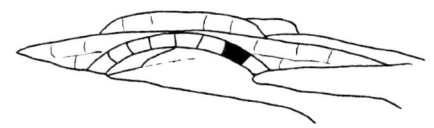

Packaging is designed primarily to protect parts or product whilst they are being transported from A to B.

However if you speak to the Sales people, they will tell you that the packaging also has a marketing aspect to it which can be a key factor in the sale of the product.

Some texts even consider the packaging to be an integral part of the product.

For this reason, we can split packaging into 4 basic types:-

Consumer Sales units (CSU)

Packaging which protects the product whilst it is on the shelf and is used to influence the customer in his purchase.

Sales units (SU)

Packaging that groups together various Consumer Sales units

Combination units (CU)

Packaging which is used to protect the product whilst it is moved

Handling units (HU)

Handling units groups together several packaging units so they can be transported more efficiently.

In certain cases the combination unit and the handling unit may be the same.

A good example to understand the difference between each one is that of batteries. When we buy a battery they often come packed in groups of 2. This is the CSU. In the shop we saw that each type of battery is grouped together in SUs. When they were shipped to the shop, the shop owner bought several SUs of the same battery and they cam in a CU. The factory, however, sold the batteries to wholesalers by the pallet (HU) of several CUs.

But we must not lose the spirit behind each of these fundamental definitions for pachaging:-

protection of what is inside whilst it is moved or stored

presentation of what is inside to help influence the decision of a prospective 'buyer'.

If we understand these 2 basic concepts of Packaging then we can see that the Packaging element is not only applicable to products or parts but also to all the other elements.

Paperwork

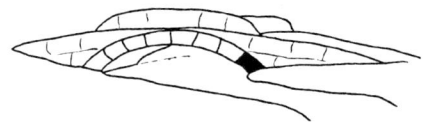

The element of paperwork relates to any documentation required. In this modern age, however, it may not actually be on paper but could be in an electronic form i.e. email, edi, e-ticket, ...

The important idea to have in mind is that the paperwork will fit into one of the following 4 categories:-

Instructive

A detailed explanation of what must be done and how. Typically these are work instructions or procedures.

Informative

Used to communicate a message to people about what is happening or about the product. These include news letters, press releases or advertisements.

Authoritative

Typically this gives authorisation for something. This could be by a governmental body or by a supervisor or parent. These could include visas, driving licences or entrance passes.

Registry

Used for the recording of activities. This could be a stamp in a passport to show entry to a country or the signature on a delivery record.

It is an element which relates very much to the other 7 elements as to what type the paperwork will be. This will be discussed in more detail in the next chapter.

Planning (Part II)

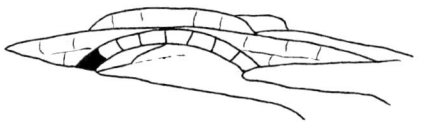

Once all the detailed activities and tasks that need to be undertaken are identified by analysing all the 8 P, we come to the second step of Planning.

All the activities and tasks need to be ordered into a workable plan. Sometimes actions take place in sequence one after the other. Other times actions will be undertaken in parallel.

These plans themselves can take many forms from simple lists of actions to more complex Gantt charts.

The plans are then communicated to all the people involved so that they know what is to be done, when and by whom.

This plan must then be monitored to ensure that the actions are completed on time and any deviation results in a corrective countermeasure to bring the global timing back on track.

The better the initial analysis, the less likely there is to be a surprise in the planning and the more likely that the overall plan will be achieved.

"Proper Prior Planning Prevents
Poor Performance"

The Next Level

The 8 P is a kind of perpetual checklist that helps identify all the details that need to be defined and controlled in order for the organisation to work correctly.

As mentioned previously, all the elements are interlinked and therefore, to ensure that every detail is thought of, this interrelationship must be explicitly verified.

To do this, a combination of the 8 P is used; for example People Placement.

In order for the phrase to sound clearer we can say "The People Placement is the Placement of the People". This allows it to be understood more easily and remove any confusion because of the English grammar.

The example of People Placement refers to how people are moved from A to B and the means of transport that would be used.

If we were to take this one step further we could say People Placement Planning i.e. the Planning for the Placement of the People. Here we are going even more in depth into the plan for moving the people from A to B.

In this chapter we will descend only one level to understand and demonstrate this thought process.

Once you have started to develop a 'Logistics Mindset', naturally you will continue to deeper and deeper levels, seeking even greater detail.

In the following brief descriptions, the aim is not to give an exhaustive list of all possibilities for each area that needs to be taken into account.

The aim is to provoke thought as to which topics could be included under each of the headings.

In some cases there is no clear explanation but only a concept that may, depending upon your type of 'Complex activity', be more or less relevant.

Stimulating your thought process by using of the 8 P will help you to develop a 'Logistics Mindset'.

This is the aim of this book.

Planning

Planning Planning

> Planning is a 2 step process. Firstly we define the goal, then we plan the tasks and activities to achieve it. Sometimes the detail is not known straight away so we can not plan everything all in one go. We must plan times when we will undertake that extra planning or plan to review the plan and make adjustments to it if necessary.

Planning Process

> How will the Planning be done? What do we need to do to create the plan? What type of plan will it be?

Planning Parts

> As stated in chapter 2, parts are an input into a Process. Be it information or physical items. In the case of planning could be the paper chart we will use to produce the Planning but also it will be the pieces of information required to undertake the Planning. This will come from the analysis of all of the 8 P. The more parts identified means more detail identified and more detail means less chance of errors occurring. (see definition of Logistics)

Planning People

> Who is going to do the Planning? What
> skills do they require? Who will monitor
> the plan once it has been defined?

Planning Product

> The Product of the Planning is the Plan.
> What form will it take?

Planning Placement

> The Placement of the Planning would
> entail getting the Planning to those who
> need it. How would this be done? Post,
> courier, fax, EDI, displaying it on the wall?

Planning Packaging

> The Packaging of the Planning links to the
> 2 basic concepts of Packaging discussed
> earlier. This could be to protect it whilst it
> is sent to somebody or to present the plan
> and get people to agree to it.

Planning Paperwork

> What Paperwork is needed for the
> Planning or the Plan? Does it require
> official approval (as in the case of say a
> building project)?

Process

Process Planning

> Process Planning refers to the detailed
> Planning of the Process.

Process Process

> Process we defined earlier as what
> transforms the Parts into Product.
> Therefore Process Process is breaking that
> transformation down into sub elements,
> step by step actions, operation by
> operation, machine by machine.

Process Parts

> The Parts of the Process could be the
> consumables that were described in
> chapter 2. This could also help remind us
> of the parts in general that will be the
> input into the Process.

Process People

> Who are the People that undertake the
> operation or operate the Process? Who are
> the People who maintain the machines?

Process Product

> This helps to remind us of the Product in
> general that will be the output of the

Process. Additionally we need to consider the other Products that a Process produces; scrap, waste, noise, fumes, heat, etc etc. It is important that these Products are also dealt with correctly.

Process Placement

Where should we place the Process for it to be in the best position? How do we move the Process there? Do we need special means of transport to move the Process or can it be just displaced by itself? In the agricultural industry the process machine has to be moved from field to field to be able to work effectively.

Process Packaging

Sometimes a Process has to be moved and Packaging may be used to protect the machines while they are being transported.

Process Paperwork

The Paperwork of the Process could relate to the works instructions in order to undertake to steps of the Process or instructions on how to run and/or maintain the machines.

Parts

Parts Planning

> This aspect relates to the Planning of the
> Parts required. An example that everyone
> can relate to is Planning what ingredients
> to buy in the supermarket for the cooking
> of tonight's meal.

Parts Process

> What is the Process of getting the Parts to
> where they are required? It's the step by
> step breakdown of all the actions required.

Parts Parts

> In many organisations, the Parts that will
> be used to produce the Product are, in
> themselves, made up of many other Parts.
> These sub Parts are often identified in the
> lower levels of the bills of materials and
> may be managed by ourselves in sub-
> Processes or by subcontractors.

Parts People

> These People could be those who do the
> Planning for the Parts, those that move the
> Parts, those that check the Parts, ...

Parts Product

Ideally, the Product of the Parts is the Product itself after it has passed through the Process.

Parts Placement

How will we get the Parts from A to B? and B to C? etc etc All the way up to where the parts will be consumed in the Process.

Parts Packaging

The Packaging of the Parts is an important element in order to ensure that the Parts get from A to B without damage in the most convenient way. Here we must not only think about the Packaging during the Placement phase from the supplier to us but also right up to the point of consumption.

Parts Paperwork

Do the Parts need any special Paperwork during the Placement? to ensure the quality level? to explain how they should be handled or stored? ...?

People

People Planning

>The Planning of the People refers to who needs to be where, when and to do what?

People Process

>The People Process could include how we recruit, train and manage people.

People Parts

>The Parts of the People. If we look at this as Parts being the input into the People element then we could refer to food, training, information, ... whatever is required by the People for them to undertake their work.

People People

>Sometimes People require supervision or to be supported by others. They could range from medical support to canteen staff, the Human Resources department to Butlers.

People Product

>The Product of the People would refer to the work that they achieve. If they are Placement People then their product would be to ensure the Placement takes place on

time without any problems. If they are Process People then they will ensure that the Process functions correctly.

People Placement

How do we get the People from A to B safely and on time?

People Packaging

People who work in certain environments need to be protected whilst they undertake the work. Are any safety clothes or equipment required? If we are going for an interview then our Packaging would be to help 'sell us' to the recruitment officer. In certain organisations there is a 'standard packaging' for the employees i.e. a uniform

People Paperwork

The Paperwork of the People could entail passports, Social Security documents, Residence or Work permits, driving licences, ...

Product

Product Planning

> The Planning of the Product would refer to the detailed Planning of what we will do with the Product once it has been produced.

Product Process

> The Process of the Product is the detail of the Process the final Product will go through.

Product Parts

> In a certain respect the Parts of the Product are the Parts element but it helps us focalise on what are the Parts that make up the Product as opposed to other Parts that could be linked to the Process i.e. the consumables mentioned earlier.

Product People

> The People of the Product are those who will be involved in handling the product or selling the Product as opposed to those that could be involved in the Parts (Parts People) or in the Process (Process People)

Product Product

> The Product of the Product is a satisfied
> Customer !

Product Placement

> The Placement of the Product is the
> movement of the finished item to where it
> is required next.

Product Packaging

> This refers to the Packaging of the Product.
> Be it Packaging for presentation, for
> movement or just protection

Product Paperwork

> Is there any Paperwork required with the
> Product? Instructions for use? Handling
> instructions? Guarantee documents?

Placement

Placement Planning

> This section refers to the detailed Planning
> of the different aspects of Placement.

Placement Process

> As mentioned earlier, often Processes need
> to be broken down into smaller steps.
> Placement is such a Process that it is full
> of sub-Placements. Here we may also refer
> to the type of Placement means i.e. car,
> plane, forklift truck, etc.

Placement Parts

> Firstly we must define what it is we are
> going to move. Then if there are other
> inputs required prior to the Placement
> Process starting.

Placement People

> Placement People could be drivers of cars
> or lorries, airline pilots or material
> handlers inside the factory. Anyone who is
> required to move something or someone.

Placement Product

Ideally, the Product of the Placement is that something or someone is in place B and no longer in place A.

Placement Placement

Sometimes the method of transport is not in the place it is required in order to start the desired journey and it must be moved there. Another example is that a lorry may have to be moved on a ferry in order for it to cross water in order to continue its journey.

Placement Packaging

The Packaging of the Placement refers in detail to packaging that's sole purpose is the protection of the Product or Parts during the Placement activity.

Placement Paperwork

The Paperwork for any Placement or journey could include tickets, passports, visas, customs papers, security passes, ...

Packaging

Packaging Planning

> The Planning of the Packaging is to plan all the steps and actions that are detailed below in the Packaging element.

Packaging Process

> The Packaging Process could be the steps of Packaging. How is it done and what Packaging machines are to be used.

Packaging Parts

> The Parts of the Packaging could include the elements that make it up i.e. the cardboard, the plastic wraps, polystyrene balls, ...

Packaging People

> Who are the People who will do the Packaging?

Packaging Product

> Ideologically, the Product of the Packaging is ensuring what is inside is free from damage in the case of protective Packaging. In the case of presentation Packaging, the Product will be a buyer influenced to 'buy' the Product inside.

Packaging Placement

The Placement of the Packaging is getting the Packaging to where it is required for when it is required.

Packaging Packaging

Sales units, combination units and handling units by definition are Packaging Packaging as they pack together several sub-modules of Packaging. Also Packaging when it is purchased come in packs protected by an outer Packaging to prevent damage before it is used.

Packaging Paperwork

The documents that could be linked to the Packaging are labels, Packaging instructions, handling instructions, etc.

Paperwork

Paperwork Planning

> The Planning of the Paperwork is to plan all the steps and actions that are detailed below.

Paperwork Process

> What is the Process for doing the Paperwork? Are any machines required to produce the Paperwork?

Paperwork Parts

> What are the Parts that make up the Paperwork? What do I need to know in order to do the Paperwork?

Paperwork People

> Who are the People to do the Paperwork?

Paperwork Product

> The product of the Paperwork depends upon the type of Paperwork itself. For example, if the Paperwork is instructive then the Product of the Paperwork is that someone can follow the instructions correctly without error.

Paperwork Placement

> How do we transport the Paperwork to
> where it is required, when it is required?

Paperwork Packaging

> The Packaging of the Paperwork may be an
> envelope, binder, folder or even a tube that
> is used for holding pictures or drawings.

Paperwork Paperwork

> In many cases we have to fill out
> application forms, give certificates and
> other documents before we get the
> Paperwork that we require.

Practical examples

In any learning process, the best way is to go through a couple of practical examples.

Each of these examples will require the use of the 8 P to help identify the detail that is required in order to achieve each objective.

Remember, if you can think of even more detail than that which is identified here then you are well on your way to developing a Logistics Mindset.

Only by applying the 8 P every day to each logistical problem that we are faced with will this become an automatic reflex.

Apply it today on simple issues so that step by step you will develop a Logistics Mindset that will assist you in the careful organisation of any complex activity that you will encounter.

Example 1

The logistical problem that needs to be resolved in this first example is a problem where only the first level will be applied.

To help the analysis we will use the form that is in Annexe 1 – The 8 P Analysis. This file is available for free download on the website www.logisticsmindset.com

The problem is that it is my wife's birthday tomorrow. My son and I have decided we will bake for her a surprise birthday cake for her party that will be held tomorrow evening at 8 Pm. To help us resolve this organisational problem we will now apply the 8 P.

The first step is Planning the goal. Defining clearly what it is we need to achieve and why.

Planning I - *The GOAL*

What : *Birthday cake*	Who : *My son and I*
When : *Tomorrow 8pm*	How many : *1*
Where : *At home*	Why : *My wife's birthday party*

After we have done this we continue to brainstorm all the 8 P and place them in the Matrix. The more detail we can think of the better.

The section Planning II in this example will then be used to prepare a short plan (itself an element of Planning) of all the other items identified. They will be organised so that the plan can be followed easily. The person who is responsible to undertake the action and when it will be undertaken must be detailed.

Once we execute the planning as defined, we can check off each item previously identified to ensure that they were used or undertaken correctly as planned.

By using the 8 P to help identify the detail of your complex activity you will stimulate your Logistics Mindset.

It is important to organise this detail into the different sections as it will help this thought process.

Write down each item identified. This way it will not be forgotten. It will not be assumed. It will be explicitly identified and thus ensure it is taken into account.

Remember - If an element is not analysed sufficiently and not taken into account then the arch will have a weak element and the bridge may collapse.

On the following page we can see the result of this first example.

The 8P Analysis

Planning I - The GOAL

What : Birthday cake
When : Tomorrow 8pm
Where : At home

Who : My son and I
How many : 1
Why : My wife's birthday party

Parts

	check
200g self raising flour	
4 eggs	
200g butter	
200g sugar	
icing sugar and water	
lots of candles and candle holders	

Process

	check
prepare ingredients	
mix together in mixing bowl	
bake in oven	
ice cake	

Product

	check
birthday cake	
smile on wife's face !!!! and happy son	

Paperwork

	check
Recipe	
birthday card and envelope	

Packaging

	check
baking tin	
cake stand	

Placement

	check
carry by hand	
walk to shop	
present cake to wife	

People

My son
Myself

what	who
buy ingredients	Me
prepare ingredients	Son
mix in mixing bowl	Son
heat oven	Me
pour into baking tin and bake in oven	Me
leave to cool	Me

Planning II

what	when	who	when	who
mix icing sugar	12h00	Me	18h30	Son
ice cake	13h00	Son	18h45	Son
place on candle	14h00	Son	19h00	Son
light candles	14h00	Me	19h59	Son
present to wife	14h30	Me	20h00	Son
blow out candles	15h00	Me	20h02	Wife

Example 2

In this second example we will tackle a more complex logistical problem relating to a manufacturing environment.

To help us do this, we will use both forms in the Annexes 1 and 2.

Once we have clearly defined the overall Plan, we will then start to investigate all the 8 P linked to this logistical problem. It is recommended to start with Process, Parts and Product going deeper into each one (to the next level) to help identify all the required detail.

As we run through this example, we will practice the reiterative approach that was discussed earlier in the book and demonstrate the thought process used to analyse this problem using the 8 P of a Logistics Mindset. This thought process will be shown as the text that is in italics in the smaller font size in the following pages.

Remember to note down all the detail identified into the matrix from Annexe 2.

So lets go!

Our logistical problem this time is the following:-

Its Monday morning at 9h00 and my company has just received a special order for 7200 logo printed golf balls that needs to be delivered to the customer before midday on Friday. This customer is nearly 600 miles away so we would have to produce and despatch all the balls before midday on Thursday in order for them to arrive on time. Sometimes these 'good news' orders that arrive on Monday morning are not as simple as they might seem. We must give a reply to the customer to say we can meet this special order if it is possible so lets get to work and check whether it is achievable or not.

The first step is always to clearly define the overall Plan i.e. the Goal. Below, we can see this defined from the information provided in the text above. If the information is insufficient then it is important that we seek out the missing information in order to clearly define this overall plan. Remember without this being clearly defined we will lose focus.

Planning I - *The GOAL*			
What :	Printed Logo Golf Balls	Who :	Customer X
When :	Friday 12h00	How many :	7200 balls
Where :	Scotland	Why :	Special Order

Now we will start with the Process element.

Process

The process itself is a printing process with a printing machine. It is a semi automatic machine as balls are loaded and unloaded manually.

Process Parts

To correctly print golf balls we need ink and a stencil for the machine.

Process Product

This process has several products. These include the printed balls but also waste ink (which we will have to dispose of correctly), heat (in some cases this can cause the machine itself to overheat), and 1% approx. of balls are rejected due to printing errors.

Process Planning

The process prints 1 ball every 15 seconds. To print 7200 balls we need, we will have to print more balls to allow for a 1% reject level. Mathematically this we be 7273 balls but as the process is never exactly 1% we will prepare to print 7300 and stop sooner if the balls are without problems. The time required therefore is 30.5 hours. As we work 8 hours per day we will need 4 days to complete the task.

Already this is a problem as between Monday midday and the time when the customer requires the product there is only 4 days and we have not talked about delivery yet. (we will come back to this point later)

Process People

As mentioned earlier the process is semi automatic so I will need an operator to operate the machine. (we will come back to this point later also)

Process Paperwork

The paperwork required for the printing machine includes the works instructions for operating it; the auto maintenance instructions to clean the machine that indicates that the machine needs to be cleaned prior to stopping for a break or at the end of the shift; and the works order which tells the operator the setup for the job.

Parts

In general, the parts for this activity are the golf balls and the ink required for the printing.

Parts Planning

As indicated in the process planning, we estimated that we will need 7300 balls. In stock we have on 3823. Therefore we will have to plan to purchase more balls. These balls come from our supplier in batches of 6000 so we will order 1 batch of 6000 balls. There is sufficient stock of ink.

Parts Placement

The parts come from a supplier who can deliver them to us for before 10am on Tuesday morning using his local van delivery service. (As the 3823 balls will keep the process running for 16 hours approx. a delivery on Tuesday at 10am should be fine.)

Parts People

The people that will order the parts are the people in the purchasing department. Those that will off load the lorry are in the Goods Inward department, who will then take them to the area beside the press for printing.

Parts Paperwork

To order the parts we will send a purchase order and then they will arrive with a delivery note and, of course, the invoice.

Parts Packaging

The parts will come as 3 balls in a sleeve. Then 2000 sleeves in a container.

Product

The product is the printed logo golf balls.

Product Packaging

The parts will be packaged 3 balls in a sleeve and 24 sleeves in a box. A total of 100 boxes. The sleeves will be the original sleeves reused but for the 100 boxes we need to check we have them available. The packaging in the sleeves is done as the balls leave the machine then the packaging operator (Packaging People or more correctly Product Packaging People) will place the sleeves into the boxes, seal the boxes and prepare the next box. Each box will be identified with a delivery address label of the customer (Product Packaging Paperwork)

Product Placement

The delivery will take place by our delivery van that will deliver the product 22 hours after it departs the factory at an average of 50mph allowing for breaks etc. If we place 2 drivers then this could be reduced to 12 hours.

Product Paperwork

The Product will be delivered with a delivery note and a copy of the invoice. The paperwork will be placed in one of the boxes clearly identified.

At this point it comes quite clear that the printing time plus the delivery time is greater than the time available. However, if we work 12 hour days instead of 8 hour days then we can dispatch on time with only one driver and the product will arrive Friday morning.

So we have to deal with the People element. In fact we are focusing in on the Process People and Product Packaging People elements identified earlier and adjusting what we previously defined.

People

As we can see above the order is possible if only we can ensure that the operators (printing and packing) will work 12 hours per day. A 12 hour shift for an individual is acceptable but we must clearly communicate the Goal to the personnel so that they understand the importance of them changing their working hours for Tuesday and Wednesday. Assuming that this was agreed we continue on. If not agreed we must investigate other solutions.

People Planning

As the team is prepared to change their working times this week, we plan that the printer and packer will work on Tuesday and Wednesday from 8h00 until 20h00. This increase will allow us sufficient time on Thursday morning to print the last few balls, print the paperwork, load the lorry and drive the product to the customer.

People Placement

We need to check that the printer and the packer do not have any difficulty in returning from work at this new time. If so, then we will have to arrange transport for them.

Process Planning

Now that the team has agreed to work the 12 hours Tuesday and Wednesday we can re-plan the process. So we start at midday on Monday and run up until 17h00. That will produce 1200 balls. Then Tuesday and Wednesday 2880 each day as the breaks will be covered by other personnel. On Thursday we will have to produce the remaining 340 balls approx. and that will take about 1.5 hours depending on reject levels.

The matrix below shows a summary of all the points so far identified. If we so wish, we could continue to search for even greater detail and this would improve our probability of success.

The 8P Matrix

	Planning	Process	Parts	People	Product	Packaging	Placement	Paperwork
Planning				Production planners and Sales team	The Plan		Fax order to Supplier Display The Plan on Team Board	Paper Gantt chart
Process	240 balls/hour 7200 / 1.01 = 7273 7300 / 240 = 30.5 hrs Mon 5hrs = 1200 balls Tue & Wed = 5600 balls Thurs balance	Semi automatic printing machine Quality Check	Ink Stencil Balls	Machine operator	Printed golf balls 1% rejects Waste ink Heat			Works intructions Works Order Maintenance Instruction Quality Control Sheet
Parts	3823 - 7300 = -3477 order 6000 delivery Tuesday before 17h00 to ensure no stoppage			Purchasing department Goods Inwards		3 balls / sleeve 2000 sleeves / container	Supplier Van Tuesday 10h00	Purchase Order Delivery Note Invoice
People	Mon -> 17h Tues 8h -> 20h Wed 8h -> 20h Thur normal hours			Coverage for meal breaks			Taxi ?	
Product				Packaging operator Van driver		3 balls / sleeve 24 sleeves / box => 100 boxes	Delivery Van 22 hours or 12 hours	Delivery Note Invoice
Placement	600 miles @ 50 mph 12 hours non stop or 22 hours with breaks	Load van and drive to Scotland		Supplier Van driver Company Van driver(s)				Driving licence for Driver Petrol money
Packaging	100 boxes	In line with the printing 3 balls / sleeve 24 sleeves / box	Sleeves	Packaging operator		Boxes	From warehouse to line	Address labels
Paperwork	Print delivery note and invoice Thursday 10h00			Despatch department		Place Invoice in one box clearly identified	Fax order to Supplier Place Invoice in one box Delivery Note hand given by driver	

At this point we have identified sufficient detail to put our initial planning together. As this allows us to achieve our goal we will now inform the customer that we accept his order then off we go. This planning must now be tracked and if we deviate from this plan then we must take the appropriate corrective actions.

The Logo Golf Ball Planning

What	Who
Create internal Works Order for the Job	Sales
Prepare printing process	Prod
Print Golf balls, check quality and pack	1200 Prod
	2880 Prod
	2880 Prod
	340 Prod
Order batch of new ball	Purch
Receive new balls	Goods In
Place in production area	Goods In
Prepare despatch paperwork	Despatch
Load lorry	Despatch
Transport of Finished Product to Customer	Transport
Tel. driver to check status of delivery	Sales
Tel. Customer to ensure that delivery arrived OK	Sales

Timescale : each time block represents 2hours starting at time indicated

Acknowledgements

Writing a book is a very challenging task and often the dream of many. In making this dream a reality, many people have contributed in their own small way. Most, until they see these pages in print, will be unaware that they have influenced the outcome of this book.

Having that initial idea is only the beginning. Putting pen to paper and structuring those thoughts is not only a time consuming exercise but also one which is very frustrating. Converting the images and words in one's head and communicating the message clearly through diagrams and text is often repeated several times until the feeling is right.

During a business trip to Cincinnati, 2 gentlemen gave that first encouragement by saying that we all have at least one good book inside us; that the world is waiting for us to tell our story or to share our thoughts. I thank them for giving me that final push to get this project underway.

In putting together the examples, we must always seek inspiration from real life experiences. In the early days of my career, I have had the pleasure to have 2 mentors, who together have shared their passions and views on both professional and personal life. Together we have been involved in many logistical issues and with a combination of their skills and vision, we have always been able to find a workable solution. Messrs Smith and Rees are prime examples of coaches giving back to the industry that they love and both have been the inspiration for many of their fellow colleagues.

Why the story of golf? Firstly, the idea of a story was chosen because people have different ways to learn. Some are artistic and some are scientific. Some are left brained and some are right brained. The idea of incorporating a story in the book was to help the widest possible audience to understand the 8 P as it is not a business or scientific tool. As explained in the story we can all benefit from developing a Logistics Mindset.

Golf, on the other hand, is a sport in which many millions of people indulge across the world. It is a game that is both social and competitive. It requires the individual to master every aspect of the game with meticulous attention to detail and therefore becomes a challenge of personal development. Its use in the story is not a coincidence but a demonstration that the 8 P really are universal.

The beautiful painting of the "Swilken Bridge towards the R&A at St. Andrews" was used for the cover illustration following the kind permission of the artist William Grandison.

To my friends and family, who have already been named throughout the text of the story, I thank you all for your encouragement along life's journey.

To the best of friends, Tim, T and MJ, I give a special thank you as true friends are so few and far between.

And finally to Cris, for her continued support not only for me to be able to complete this project but also for all the other projects we have undertaken together and for that which started unexpectedly on Christmas Day 2004 - Martin.

About the Author

NIGEL WING

Son to Val and Stan, husband to Cris and father to Martin.

Nigel Wing graduated from Hatfield Polytechnic in Manufacturing System Engineering. Having started his career in production systems within the automotive industry, he was soon attracted into the world of Logistics and Supply Chain Management.

When asked what his strengths are, his reply was: "Patience, Perseverance, attention to detail and a sense of humour."

His career has taken him around the world several times but his mind can often be seen drifting down the fairway of a golf course.

Email nigelwing@logisticsmindset.com
Website www.logisticsmindset.com

Logistics Mindset

About the cover artist

WILLIAM GRANDISON

Grandison Golf Gallery produces the highest quality limited edition prints of the world's premier golf courses.

William Grandison graduated from Edinburgh College of Art and is internationally recognised as one of the world's leading golf landscape artists.

His individual style and attention to detail have earned him numerous awards, and his paintings and prints, now highly collectable, adorn many of golf's most prestigious venues. This highly acclaimed artist's work can be found in the private collections of many prominent figures of entertainment and sport, including Arnold Palmer, Tom Watson and Max Faulkner.

William is an honorary member of the spectacular Old Head Golf Links in Ireland.

For more information contact William at:

GRANDISON GOLF GALLERY
Gowanbank, 5 Sorley's Brae, Dollar, FK14 7AS, Scotland
Tel (44) 01259 740318 - Fax (44) 01259 740318
Email info@grandisongolfgallery.com
Website www.grandisongolfgallery.com

Annexe 1 – The 8 P Analysis

The 8P Analysis

Planning I - *The GOAL*		Who : How many : Why :
What : When : Where :		

Parts	check	Process	check	Product	check

Paperwork	check	Packaging	check	Placement	check

People		Planning II			
check	what	when	what	who	when
		who		when	

Annexe 2 – The 8 P Matrix

The 8P Matrix

	Planning	Process	Parts	People	Product	Packaging	Placement	Paperwork
Planning								
Process								
Parts								
People								
Product								
Placement								
Packaging								
Paperwork								

ISBN 1-41204837-0